T0413589

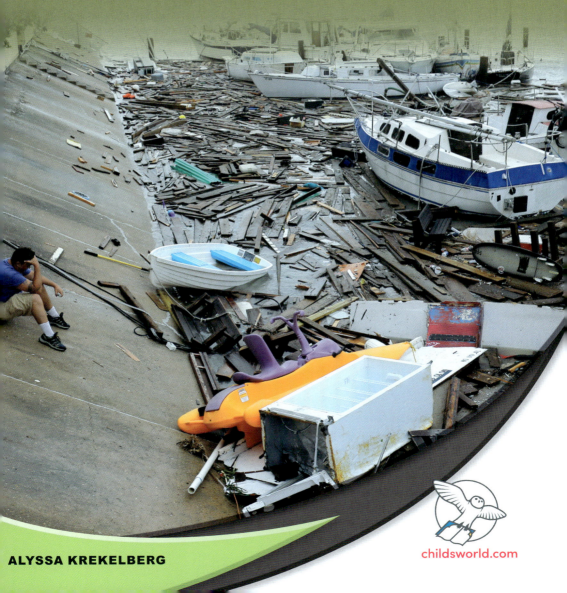

HURRICANE
SURVIVAL STORIES

ALYSSA KREKELBERG

childsworld.com

ABOUT THE AUTHOR

Alyssa Krekelberg writes and edits books for young readers. She lives in Minnesota with her husband, daughter, and hyper husky.

childsworld.com

Published by The Child's World®
800-599-READ • www.childsworld.com

Photography Credits
Photographs ©: Eric Gay/AP Images, cover, 1; Shutterstock Images, 5, 15, 18 (top), 18 (top middle), 18 (middle), 18 (bottom middle); Lieut. Commander Mark Moran/NOAA, 6; Mike Groll/AP Images, 10; Gerry Broome/AP Images, 13; Red Line Editorial, 14, 23, 28; Lt. Zachary West/US Department of Defense, 16; Nadezhda Shoshina/Shutterstock Images, 18 (bottom); Petty Officer 3rd Class Johanna Strickland/ US Department of Defense, 19; Alessandro Pietri/ Shutterstock Images, 20; Ramon Espinosa/AP Images, 22; Rebecca Blackwell/AP Images, 24; Zern Liew/Shutterstock Images, 25; Robert Michaud/ iStockphoto, 26

ISBN Information
9781503854543 (Reinforced L brary Binding)
9781503854826 (Portable Document Format)
9781503855205 (Online Multi-user eBook)
9781503855588 (Electronic Publication)

LCCN 2023937076

Printed in the United States of America

CONTENTS

WHAT IS A HURRICANE?

A hurricane is a powerful storm that forms over warm ocean waters near the **equator**. It starts as a weather event such as a **tropical wave** or thunderstorm. The event may continually suck up warm, moist air. As the moist air rises, it cools and releases water. This forms clouds. As the air keeps rising, it begins to rotate. The storm becomes a hurricane if winds reach 74 miles per hour (119 kmh) or more.

People have different names for this type of storm. If it's in the Atlantic Ocean, the storm is called a hurricane. In other areas, people call it a tropical cyclone or typhoon.

In the Atlantic, hurricane season is between June 1 and November 30. During late summer, ocean waters are at their warmest temperatures. Hurricanes are most likely to form during this time. On average, seven hurricanes develop in the Atlantic every year. Not all of them make landfall, or reach land. When hurricanes reach land, they can bring damaging winds, tornadoes, rain, and **storm surges**. People's lives may be at risk if they are caught in a hurricane.

FAST FACTS

- ▶ Hurricane Katrina made landfall at Plaquemines Parish, Louisiana, on August 29, 2005. Approximately 1,392 people were killed.

- ▶ Hurricane Sandy barreled across the Caribbean Sea, hitting New Jersey on October 29, 2012. About 147 people died.

- ▶ Hurricane Harvey slammed into Port Aransas, Texas, on August 25, 2017, killing 89 people.

- ▶ Hurricane Maria reached Puerto Rico on September 20, 2017. Around 2,975 people in Puerto Rico died.

- ▶ Hurricane Ian struck Cayo Costa, Florida, on September 28, 2022, eventually killing 148 people.

CHAPTER ONE

GETTING OUT ALIVE

Andre grabbed his wife and son as water began pushing into their house. They rushed to the second floor as water rose behind them, swallowing the stairs. The **levees** in New Orleans, Louisiana, had broken after Hurricane Katrina slammed into the area on August 29, 2005. As a result, the city was flooding.

Andre and his family were trapped. The lights flickered out, and the water continued to rise. It was up to Andre's waist before it finally stopped. He pushed his way onto the balcony and saw that his neighborhood was mostly underwater. Shouts filled the night air. "People [were] yelling, banging on the roofs of houses from the inside. They'd climbed up to get away from the water and got themselves stuck in their attics with no way to break out," Andre said.

In the morning, a boat came to rescue people from the neighborhood. Andre and his family were dropped off at an **overpass**. Hundreds of people were already there, and hardly anyone had food. People waited for help, hoping to go to a safer place. But no help came.

Some people on the overpass began stealing what they could from others. Andre worried for his family's safety. He was able to call his sister. She told Andre that her house was spared from the flooding brought by Hurricane Katrina. She had electricity and running water. She told Andre to come over to her house as soon as he could.

But Andre had no way to escape the water surrounding the overpass. His wife couldn't swim. Neither could his young son.

HURRICANE CATEGORIES

Hurricanes are categorized based on their wind speeds. Anything higher than a category 2 is considered a major hurricane. Hurricane Katrina made landfall as a category 3. The storm had winds of up to 125 miles per hour (201 kmh).

Category	Wind Speeds	Damage Caused
1	74 to 95 miles per hour (119–153 kmh)	• Homes may have some damage to their siding or roofs. • Large tree branches may break. • Some trees may be blown down. • Damaged power lines could leave people without electricity for days.
2	96 to 110 miles per hour (154–177 kmh)	• Homes may have major damage to their siding and roofs. • Trees may be ripped from the ground and block roads. • Power may be out for a few days or weeks.
3	111 to 129 miles per hour (179–208 kmh)	• Homes may have major damage such as roofs being destroyed. • Many trees will be damaged and blown down. • Water and electricity may not be available for a few days or weeks.
4	130 to 156 miles per hour (209–251 kmh)	• Homes may lose their walls or roofs. • The majority of trees will be damaged. • Many power lines will be down and people won't have electricity for weeks.
5	157 miles per hour (253 kmh) or more	• Most houses will be destroyed and most trees will be damaged. • The power will be out for weeks or months.

Then he saw a man with an air mattress. "I went to him and I says, 'Look, man, I got to get my family out of here. . . . I want to ask you to loan me that air mattress. Please,'" Andre said. The man handed over the air mattress without a word.

Andre and his family went to the edge of the water. His wife and son sat on top of the air mattress while Andre pushed them forward. Soon the water was up to his neck. He walked for hours in the direction of his sister's house. He saw dead people in the water. During the storm and in the days after, more than 1,300 people died. Approximately 275,000 homes were destroyed or damaged because of Hurricane Katrina. New Orleans suffered the most from the storm. But the city didn't get directly hit by Katrina's strong winds. Most of the destruction in the city was caused by Katrina's rain and storm surge, which the city's levees couldn't handle. Eighty percent of the city flooded as a result.

Andre and his family reached his sister's house. They eventually went to North Carolina. But once it was safe, Andre and his family returned to New Orleans. Andre began working as a delivery person and spoke with people about their experiences during the storm. He also looked for ways to make people's lives easier. "I go out of my way to find somebody [who] needs something, every day. And I try to help, help somebody every day. Makes me feel good," he said.

CHAPTER TWO

SURVIVING SANDY

The howling wind from Hurricane Sandy terrified Pamela Vazquez, who was at home with her husband, Bob, and their dog, Molly. It was October 29, 2012, and the storm had made landfall in New Jersey. Vazquez looked outside and saw a terrifying sight: the houses across the street weren't there anymore. Then a loud crash came from her own home as the storm tore off the deck stairs. Water from the nearby bay filled her Union Beach neighborhood.

Suddenly, the house gave a sickening lurch. It had been ripped from its foundation and was floating in the raging waters, heading directly toward a large tree. When the house and tree collided, Vazquez, Bob, and Molly were tossed into the water.

Vazquez held Molly tightly by the leash. But Molly weighed about 80 pounds (36 kg), and she was beginning to panic.

◄ Hurricane Sandy damaged or destroyed more than 300,000 homes in New Jersey.

She kept pulling Vazquez under the waves. Vazquez gasped for breath. She was on the verge of drowning.

"You have to let go!" Bob begged from beside her. But Vazquez held on, not wanting to lose her dog to the storm. Soon Vazquez's strength faded, and the leash slipped out of her hand. Molly was carried away by the waves. "She was gone," Bob later recalled.

The couple needed to get somewhere safe. Most of the houses around them were gone. **Debris** from destroyed homes filled the water. Trees and cars floated in the water, too. The smell of gasoline from cars filled the air. But one neighbor's house was still standing. Vazquez and Bob fought the floodwaters, trying to get to it.

A piece of debris smacked Vazquez in the head. She fell underneath the water, and pain pierced her skull. Then she felt someone tugging on her hair. Bob had reached beneath the waves and grabbed her. He pulled her to the surface. The two kept making their way to the nearby house, but Vazquez was in pain and exhausted. When they reached the deck of the house, she was too weak to climb onto it. Bob yanked her up out of the water, and they rolled onto the deck.

The couple inside the house took them in. They gave Vazquez and Bob dry clothes. They told Vazquez to rest in bed.

Hundreds of pets were lost or left behind ▶ during Hurricane Sandy. Some people helped rescue pets affected by the storm.

HURRICANE SANDY'S PATH

Hurricane Sandy caused damage to many countries, including Jamaica, Cuba, Haiti, the Bahamas, and the United States. It started in the Caribbean Sea on October 22, 2012, as a tropical storm. It ended after hitting New Jersey.

October 29: Sandy makes landfall in New Jersey.

October 25: Sandy hits the Bahamas.

October 25: Sandy makes landfall in Cuba and Haiti.

October 24: Sandy hits Jamaica as a category 1 hurricane.

October 22: A tropical storm forms. The National Hurricane Center names it Sandy.

▲ After Hurricane Sandy, many people
volunteered to help clean up debris.

She collapsed onto the mattress as the storm continued to
rage outside.

Bob was with his neighbors when one of them called out,
"Look, there's a dog out there!" Molly had made her way back to
them, holding on to a piece of floating wood. One of the neighbors
hurried outside and grabbed her. Then Molly went to find Vazquez.
The family was reunited in the middle of the terrible storm.

Around 147 people died because of Hurricane Sandy. This
massive storm was more than 900 miles (1,448 km) wide, causing
some people to call it Superstorm Sandy. It hit multiple countries
and left around 200,000 people without homes.

CHAPTER THREE

A JOINT RESCUE

Roger Patterson looked at the flooded neighborhood before him. Some houses were completely underwater. Patterson was the squad leader for Texas Task Force 1, a water rescue team. In the wake of Hurricane Harvey, his team had been helping people escape the disastrous flooding caused by the strong storm.

Harvey hit Texas on August 25, 2017, as a category 4 hurricane. Five days later, Patterson was still trying to rescue people.

His team had gotten a call about an older couple who needed help getting out of their neighborhood. One of them was paralyzed. The Texas National Guard had transported Patterson and his team out to the couple's home. But now it was Texas Task Force 1's job to navigate the deep water.

The team approached the couple's house. Someone grabbed a kayak that was bobbing in the water nearby. The team would use it as a litter to carry the paralyzed man safely through the dirty, deep water. As they were moving the man, a volunteer in a boat pulled up and offered to help. The paralyzed man's wife needed a ride, so the volunteer brought her to a safe place where she could wait for her husband. Now members of Texas Task Force 1 could put all their attention on helping the man. They brought him back to where the Texas National Guard waited.

The man had trouble controlling his body temperature. Rain started pouring down. "We had covered him up with as many blankets as we had available, but it continued to rain and the temperature was dropping. . . . I was worried he would become hypothermic," said Matt Paul, a member of Texas Task Force 1.

A bystander hurried over, carrying two umbrellas. He held them over the man to protect him from the rain.

Patterson knew the man needed medical attention. He called for an ambulance, but medical teams were already overwhelmed with patients after Hurricane Harvey. Patterson worried an ambulance wouldn't arrive in time to help the man.

HARVEY'S IMPACT

Hurricane Harvey reached Texas on August 25, 2017. Then the storm slowed. For four days, it dumped more than 5 feet (1.5 m) of rain onto Texas. This caused a massive amount of flooding and damage.

 Harvey left **$152.5 billion** worth of damage.

 89 people died because of the storm.

 Federal troops rescued **10,000 people**. The Houston Police Department rescued another **3,000 people**.

 More than **30,000 people** had to leave the area because of the flooding.

 More than **200,000 houses and businesses** were damaged or destroyed.

▲ **Hurricane rescue teams often use helicopters to help locate and transport injured people.**

Then a helicopter appeared in the sky. It was the US Coast Guard searching for survivors. Paul got the helicopter's attention. It began circling above them—a sign that it wanted to land. The Texas National Guard members jumped into action. They cleared the area and found a safe landing spot for the helicopter. Once members of the Coast Guard were on the ground, they helped get the man and his wife onto the helicopter and took the couple to a hospital straightaway.

Martin Davila was a member of the Texas National Guard. He was part of the rescue efforts. "I'm glad we had all the support we had," he said. "It made me really proud to be a Texan."

CHAPTER FOUR

COMING TOGETHER

Phyllis Richards put a wooden board over the glass window in her living room. Then she started stacking sandbags at the bottom of the back door to cover any gaps. Richards was convinced these things would protect her house from Hurricane Maria's wind and rain as the storm barreled toward Puerto Rico.

But Richards still didn't sleep well on the night of September 20, 2017. She was worried about her two young daughters.

In the morning, Richards woke to floodwaters gushing into her home. The hurricane was dumping heavy rain onto the island and causing flooding. Richards had to get her children to a safer place as quickly as possible. She grabbed handfuls of clothes and packed some milk to drink. Then she grabbed her daughters' red life jackets to wear as they navigated the floodwaters.

Outside, Richards saw that her neighbors' house was in better shape. She took her daughters there, and the neighbors welcomed them in. But the floodwaters kept rising. They had to find shelter in a safer place. Richards, her children, and the neighbors worked their way through the storm. The sky above them was dark, and wind seemed to whip at them from all sides.

Another house opened its doors to them. Richards and her family joined a group of 14 other people who were sheltering there. Two dogs weaved around the anxious adults and children. Richards and her daughters stayed there for around six hours as Hurricane Maria battered the island. But soon the streets outside transformed into rivers, and the water kept coming. So Richards and her children had to enter the storm once again to find safety.

▲ **Many Puerto Ricans lost their homes and belongings in Hurricane Maria.**

They piled into a truck that was getting swallowed by the water. But the truck still started, so Richards and her family were able to drive through the strong winds and rain. They made it to a family member's house and waited out the storm there.

The next morning, Richards saw the destruction caused by Hurricane Maria. She went back to see her flooded house. The furniture and most of her kids' toys were ruined. Richards spent the next days looking for water and food. The grocery store had no way to get fresh supplies, so the food there was expired. There was no electricity or cell phone service.

Still, the community came together. "Our small neighborhood symbolized generosity, hope and resilience," said Richards.

"Neighbors shared chicken strips. When I cooked fresh food, whatever was left unused was shared with my neighbors." People cleaned up the area. They even washed up a dollhouse that belonged to Richards's daughters. Someone shared a generator, a machine used to make electricity, so some homes could get power.

Hurricane Maria devastated Puerto Rico. Many people were without power for months or more. More than 87,000 homes were destroyed. Experts estimate that 2,975 people on the island were killed.

COSTLIEST HURRICANES

Hurricanes can cause a lot of damage. Fixing this damage can cost a significant amount of money. As of early 2023, Hurricane Maria was the fourth-costliest hurricane in US history.

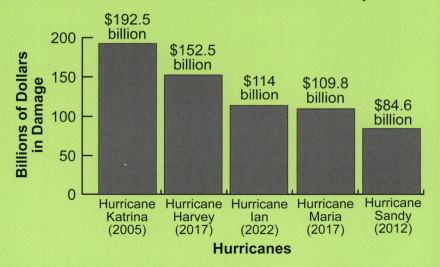

CHAPTER FIVE

AT SEA DURING A HURRICANE

As the sky darkened, David Littlefield navigated his boat through choppy ocean waters. It was September 28, 2022, and Hurricane Ian was approaching fast. Littlefield had tried to outrun the storm and failed. Now, just off the coast of Florida, Littlefield was doing everything he could to try to stay afloat.

◄ In cities along the Florida coast, Hurricane Ian damaged thousands of boats at marinas and wharfs.

The ocean water churned, and suddenly it was overtaking the boat. Littlefield was in the boat's cabin. Water pressed against the door, and Littlefield couldn't get out. His little white boat was no match for the category 4 storm. The boat began to tip to the side.

Then the waves and wind calmed. "I saw blue skies. And I said, now's the time. I gotta get out," Littlefield remembered.

PARTS OF A HURRICANE

A hurricane has three main parts: the rainbands, eyewall, and eye.

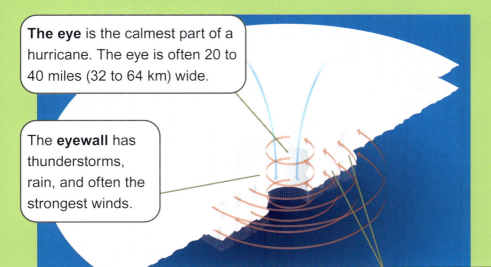

The eye is the calmest part of a hurricane. The eye is often 20 to 40 miles (32 to 64 km) wide.

The **eyewall** has thunderstorms, rain, and often the strongest winds.

Rainbands spiral away from the eyewall and are made of clouds and thunderstorms. The bands may have bursts of strong winds, heavy rain, and even tornadoes.

▲ US Coast Guard helicopters are often used after natural disasters to help locate and transport survivors.

He was in the eye of the hurricane. This is located at the center of the storm, and it's the calmest part. Winds in the eye may only be 15 miles per hour (24 kmh). The rest of the storm was battering Florida with 150-mile-per-hour (241 kmh) winds. In the calm, Littlefield squeezed through a window in the cabin and made it onto the deck of the boat. Now that he was outside, Littlefield gripped onto the boat's railing and waited to be rescued.

His emergency device sent out a call for help, but nothing could be done as the storm raged on. When the eye of the storm passed, Littlefield was once again hit with strong winds and raging waves. He spent ten hours holding onto his boat, not knowing whether he was going to survive.

Finally, the US Coast Guard received Littlefield's emergency signal. When it was safe to fly, a team set out to find him. They flew their helicopter through 52-mile-per-hour (84 kmh) winds in the dark. "We had to fly around for quite a little while," said Micah Acree, who flew the helicopter. "And then we saw his boat coming through the mist."

A rescue swimmer grabbed Littlefield and brought him to safety. The Coast Guard would also save 745 more people and 94 pets from Hurricane Ian. Approximately 148 people died because of the storm, which brought damaging winds, heavy rain, a dangerous storm surge, and flooding. Littlefield was grateful he made it through. "Sweetest sound I ever heard—that helicopter," he said.

THINK ABOUT IT

▶ People can't always leave areas that are in the path of a hurricane. List three reasons why this might happen.
▶ If you were stuck in a hurricane, what survival items would you pack for an emergency? Why would you pick these things?
▶ How can you help people who have been impacted by hurricanes?

HURRICANE MAP

CANADA

NORTH DAKOTA
SOUTH DAKOTA
NEBRASKA
KANSAS
OKLAHOMA
TEXAS
MINNESOTA
WISCONSIN
IOWA
ILLINOIS
INDIANA
MISSOURI
KENTUCKY
TENNESSEE
ARKANSAS
MISSISSIPPI
LOUISIANA
ALABAMA
MICHIGAN
OHIO
WEST VIRGINIA
VIRGINIA
NORTH CAROLINA
SOUTH CAROLINA
GEORGIA
FLORIDA
VERMONT
MAINE
NEW HAMPSHIRE
MASSACHUSETTS
RHODE ISLAND
CONNECTICUT
NEW JERSEY
DELAWARE
MARYLAND
NEW YORK
PENNSYLVANIA

N
W E
S

THE BAHAMAS
DOMINICAN REPUBLIC
CUBA
PUERTO RICO
JAMAICA
HAITI
MEXICO
BELIZE
HONDURAS
GUATEMALA
NICARAGUA
EL SALVADOR
COSTA RICA
PANAMA
ECUADOR
VENEZUELA
GUYANA
COLOMBIA
BRAZIL
PERU

Key

- 🟧 Hurricane Katrina (2005)
- 🟩 Hurricane Sandy (2012)
- 🟪 Hurricane Harvey (2017)
- 🟥 Hurricane Maria (2017)
- 🟦 Hurricane Ian (2022)

GLOSSARY

debris (duh-BREE): Pieces of things that have been destroyed or broken down are called debris. Debris was left in the storm's wake.

equator (ee-KWAY-tur): The equator is an imaginary line around the Earth. Hurricanes form over ocean waters near the equator.

hypothermic (hy-poh-THUR-mik): If someone's body loses heat more quickly than he can make it, he may become hypothermic. The rescue team worried the man would become hypothermic.

levees (LEV-eez): Levees are structures built alongside bodies of water to prevent flooding. The levees in New Orleans failed during Hurricane Katrina.

litter (LIT-uhr): A litter is a stretcher used for carrying someone who needs help. The rescue team put the man on a litter.

overpass (OH-vuhr-pass): An overpass is a bridge or road that goes over a different road. The floodwaters weren't high enough to cover the overpass.

paralyzed (PAYR-uh-lized): To be paralyzed means to be incapable of moving by oneself. The paralyzed man needed help escaping the floodwaters.

storm surges (STORM SURJ-ez): Storm surges happen during a storm when seawater rises above its normal level. Storm surges can cause severe flooding.

tropical wave (TRAH-pi-kuhl WAYV): A tropical wave is a low-pressure area in Earth's atmosphere that develops near Africa and heads west. The tropical wave developed into a hurricane.

SELECTED BIBLIOGRAPHY

"How Hurricanes Form." *UCAR*, n.d., scied.ucar.edu. Accessed 2 Mar. 2023.

Schleifstein, Mark. "How Many People Died in Hurricane Katrina? Toll Reduced 17 Years Later." *NOLA*, 15 Jan. 2023, nola.com. Accessed 2 Mar. 2023.

"What Is a Hurricane?" *National Ocean Service*, n.d., oceanservice.noaa.gov. Accessed 2 Mar. 2023.

FIND OUT MORE

BOOKS

Crane, Cody. *All about Hurricanes*. New York, NY: Children's Press, 2021.

Hudak, Heather C. *Surviving the Hurricane: Hear My Story*. New York, NY: Crabtree Publishing, 2020.

Meister, Cari. *Hurricanes*. Minneapolis, MN: Pogo Books, 2016.

WEBSITES

Visit our website for links about hurricanes:
childsworld.com/links

Note to Parents, Caregivers, Teachers, and Librarians: We routinely verify our Web links to make sure they are safe and active sites. So encourage your readers to check them out!

INDEX